Let's Marry Said the Cherry

Let's Marry Said the Cherry

And Other Nonsense Poems

WRITTEN AND ILLUSTRATED BY

N. M. Bodecker

FABER & FABER
London

First published in Great Britain 1977
by Faber and Faber Limited
3 Queen Square London WC1
Printed in Great Britain by
Redwood Burn Limited
Trowbridge & Esher

First published in United States of America in 1974

British Library Cataloguing in Publication Data

Bodecker, Nick Mogens
  Let's marry said the cherry, and other
  nonsense poems.
  I. Title
  821'.9'14   PZ8.3.B5994

  ISBN 0–571–11093–2

Contents

THE PORCUPINE

Rebecca Jane,
a friend of mine,
went out to pat
a porcupine.

She very shortly
came back in,
disgusted with
the porcupin.

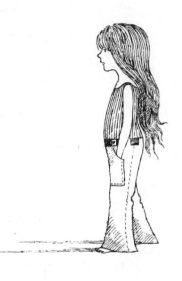

"One never, ever
should," said Jane,
"go out and pat
a porcupain!"

MR. SKINNER

Orville Skinner
(kite-string spinner)
never stopped
to eat his dinner,
for he found it
too exciting
and rewarding
to go kiting

Flying kites,
he used to sing:
"I'm a spinner
on a string!"
When they warned him:
"Mister Skinner,
capable
but high-strung spinner,
it may take you
to Brazil,"
Skinner cried:
"I hope it will!"

THE LARK IN SARK

The lark
in Sark
is known for its bark,
which is worse
than its bite,
and it bites like a shark.
Loud,
bothersome lark.

THE GEESE IN GREECE

The geese
in Greece
grow white
woolly fleece,
which is made
into shawls
in the Peloponnese.
Nice
heartwarming
geese.

IF I WERE AN ELEPHANT

If I were an elephant,
I would love my trunk.
If I were a junk man,
I would love my junk.

You don't know what a junk is?
It's an ancient Chinese craft
that's not quite like a clipper
and not quite like a raft.

If I were a ship's mate,
I would love my ship.
If I were a chipmunk,
I would love my chip.

You don't know what a chip is?
It's a little like a flake
but is more like half a sliver
and is mostly a mistake.

If I were a sparrow,
I would love to row.
If I were a potato,
I would love my toe.

You don't know what a toe is?
Well, very simply put:
it's a clumsy sort of finger
you find growing on your foot.

If I were a hatter,
I would love my hat.
If I were a batter,
I would love my bat.

You don't know what a bat is?
Now surely you have heard
it's a birdy sort of rodent
or a mousy sort of bird.

If I were a fishpond,
I would love my fish.
If I were a radish
I would love my ish.

You don't know what an ish is?
It's what that radish had
to have, because without it
it would only be a rad.

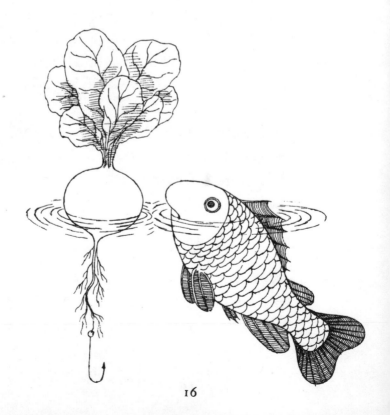

If I were an inchworm
I would love to inch.
If I were a pinchworm,
I would love to pinch.

You don't know what a pinch is?
It's something you are in
when you don't know how to finish
a poem you begin . . .

and you don't know what a junk is,
and the jumbo packed his trunk,
and the chip is on your shoulder,
and you never met a monk,
and you think you know a hatter,
but an inchworm pinched his hat,
and the bat ate up the batter
when the radish came to bat!

Well, I'm sorry for you, Charley,
you are really in a jam!
And you don't know what a jam is?
Well, it's sorry, that I am!

J. PRIOR, ESQ.

Johnson Prior
(country squire)
kept a mixed
but earnest
choir:
seven pigs,
a mule
(or donkey)
fourteen parrots,
and a monkey,
sixteen cats,
a Mr. Ford,
(Mrs. Ford on harpsichord).
When they cried:
"Oh! Johnson Prior!
Your agglomeratious
choir
is an insult to the ear!"
Squire Prior
couldn't hear.

THE ARMADILLO

While walking in the woods,
an armadillo
beheld a nest containing
a gorillo!
A nest, I mean, containing
a gorilla,
Which very much confused
that armadilla!

BENNINGTON

Find me a rhyme
for the city of Bennington:
Henington,
Wrenington,
Nowhere–and–Whenington.
Nine out of tenington
visiting Bennington
go there againington.
No one knows why.

JOHN

John could take his clothes off
but could not put them on.

His patient mother dressed him,
and said to little John,

"Now, John! You keep your things on."
But John had long since gone—

and left a trail of sneakers
and small things in the sun,

so she would know to find him
wherever he might run.

And at the end of every trail
stood Mrs. Jones & Son,

she with all his little clothes,
and little John—with none!

For John could take his clothes off
but could not put them on.

His patient mother dressed him
and on went little John—
and on—
      and on—
           and on—

THE ISLAND OF MULL

The island of Mull
is drizzly and dull.
There's sometimes a storm,
but mostly a lull.
Then nothing is heard
but the great ghastly gull,
who yawns in the mists
o'er the island of Mull.

MR. DOCER

Harry Docer
(village grocer)
shut his shutters
ever closer.
Everything
he locked in storage:
drawers full
of jam 'n' porridge,
peanut butter
wrapped in socks,
goose fat
in the money box.
When they told him:
"Mister Docer,
timid
and suspicious grocer,
this is an appalling
mess!"
Grocer Docer said:
"I guess . . ."

THE ISLAND OF RUM

The island of Rum
is exceedingly glum,
except in July
when the butterflies hum.
Humming or mum,
the butterflies come
at the end of July
to the island of Rum.

THE ISLAND OF YORRICK

The island of Yorrick
is intensely historic,
and covered with ruins
Ionic and Doric.
The people who live there
are phantasmagoric,
which means: There are ghosts
on the island of Yorrick.

MR. SLATTER

Ormsby Slatter
(crusty hatter)
made his hats
of brittle-batter.
These (as they
were most delicious,
scrumptious, and
indeed nutritious)
sold like hot cakes
through the town,

till the rain
came pouring down,
when they cried:
"Oh! Mister Slatter!
Dreadful and
deceitful hatter!
All your hats
have turned to mush."
Slatter said:
"Go home and wash!"

"LET'S MARRY!"
SAID THE CHERRY

"Let's marry,"
said the cherry.

"Why me?"
said the pea.

" 'Cause you're sweet,"
said the beet.

"Say you will,"
said the dill.

"Think it over,"
said the clover.

"Don't rush,"
said the squash.

"Here's your dress,"
said the cress.

"White and green,"
said the bean.

"And your cape,"
said the grape.

"Trimmed with fur,"
said the burr.

"Won't that tickle?"
said the pickle.

"Who knows?"
said the rose.

"Where's the chapel?"
said the apple.

"In Greenwich,"
said the spinach.

"We'll be there!"
said the pear.

"Wearing what?"
said the nut.

"Pants and coats,"
said the oats.

"Shoes and socks,"
said the phlox.

"Shirt and tie,"
said the rye.

"We'll look jolly,"
said the holly.

"You'll look silly,"
said the lily.

"You're crazy,"
said the daisy.

"Come, let's dine,"
said the vine.

"Yeah—let's eat!"
said the wheat.

"And get stout,"
aid the sprout.

"Just wait,"
said the date.

"Who will chime?"
said the lime.

"I'll chime!"
said the thyme.

"Who will preach?"
said the peach.

"It's my turn!"
said the fern.

"You would ramble,"
said the bramble.

"Here they come!"
cried the plum.

"Start the tune!"
cried the prune.

"All together!"
cried the heather.

"Here we go!"
said the sloe.

"NOW—let's marry!"
said the cherry.

"Why me?"
said the pea.

"Oh, my gosh!"
said the squash.

"Start all over,"
said the clover.

"NO WAY!"
said the hay.

THE ISLAND OF MURRAY

The island of Murray
knows never a worry.
The people who live there
are not in a hurry.
When they *do* need to rush,
they sleep in a surrey,
with a fringe on the top,
on the island of Murray.

THE ISLAND OF YARROW

The island of Yarrow
was long, low, and narrow,
too long to hoe
and too slim to harrow.
They tried with a plow,
but the sea filled the narrow
deep furrow that once
was the island of Yarrow.

MR. 'GATOR

Elevator operator
P. Cornelius Alligator,
when his passengers
were many,
never
ever
passed up
any:
when his passengers
were few,
always managed
to make do.

When they told him:
"Mister 'Gator!
quickly
in your elevator
take us
to the nineteenth floor!"
they were never
seen no more.

BOOTERIES AND FLUTERIES AND
FLATTERIES AND THINGS

If a place where they sell boots is called
a bootery,
then a place where they sell flutes must be
a flutery.
A place where they sell fish must be
a fishery,
and a china seller's shop
a cup'n'dishery.

A house that's full of flats is quite
a flattery,
but one that's full of bats is just
a battery.
A place to get your pots in is
a pottery,
but if you need a lot, you need
a lottery.

Some hospitals get nurses in a
nursery,
some pursers get their purses in
a pursery,
some people keep their grannies in
a granary
or send them for a tan to someone's
tannery

The place to keep young misses is
a missery
(but if it's his not hers it's called
a hisery).
A safe place for Miss Greene is in
a greenery,
so if she makes a scene, she's in
a scenery.

For the crocodiles are watching from
the crockery
and the mocking birds are scowling in
the mockery,
and someone's sure to trick you in
the trickery,
to make you laugh and hiccup in
the hickory,

or make you spell forever in
the spellery,
in the deepest, darkest cellar in
the celery.
So you'd better do your sums now in
the summary
and afterward stay mum in someone's
mummery,

for the actors want to put you in their
actory,
and that's a fact, in anybody's
factory.

THE SNAIL AT YALE

The snail
at Yale
likes mutton
and ale,
and passing
exams
without bother
and fail.
Snug,
old-fashioned
snail.

MISS BITTER

Sitter Bitter
(baby-sitter
Violet Amanda Bitter)
loved to sit,
but, rather sadly,
though the babies
loved her madly,
though they loved her
every bit,
never got
a chance to sit
since they found her
with her knitting,
since the day
they found her, sitting
knitting on the baby's knee,
having buttered toast and tea.

When they cried:
"AMANDA BITTER!
Most outrageous baby-sitter
BITTER! You get off that knee!"
she inquired:
"Want some tea?"

UP AND DOWN

Up stairs
and down stairs,
two simply colosserous
hippomopotami
dragged a rhinoceros.
They said: "You're ridiculous,
downright preposserous,
with that spike on your nose,
you somnambulous 'noceros."

Up hill
and down hill,
sniffing excitedly,
two timorous tapirs
tiptoed delightedly.
They said: "It's remarkable,
simply incredible,
how much of the landscape
turns out to be edible."

Up state
and down state,
a smart alligator
ran for the office
of state legislator.
He said: "If elected,
true to my nature,
I'll put teeth in your laws
—and your state legislature."

Up street
and down street,
riding relentlessly,
a mealy bug trotted
a milliped endlessly.
"Giddy up! Giddy up!"
cried the tiny equestrian,
"you ambling, rambling
millipedestrian!"

Up stream
and down stream,
two grinning gorillas
patiently paddled
their upturned umbrellas.
They cried, in a splatter
of giggles and gurgles:
"How grand to be moving
in nautical circles!"

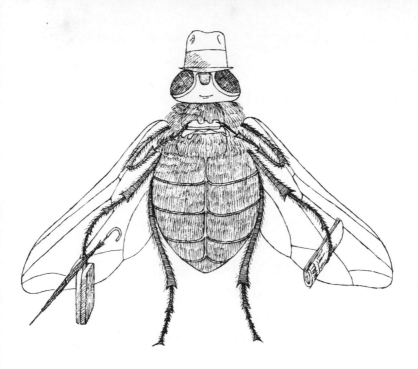

THE FLY IN RYE

The fly
in Rye
is a regular guy
who eats nothing
whatever
but roast beef
on rye.
Good,
regular guy.

MR. WELLER

Upton Weller
(senior teller)
kept a boa
in his cellar,
which, when it got hungry,
grumbled
fretfully
and roared and rumbled:
"Where's my roast beef?
Where's my ham?
Where's my little
leg of lamb?"
When they cried:
"Oh! Mister Weller!
Such alarums
in your cellar!
Are you all right
Mister Well. . . ."
Teller Weller
couldn't tell.

THE ISLAND OF LLINCE

The island of Llince
is covered in chintz
printed in patterns
of rhubarb and quince.
The King who once lived there
has not been seen since
they wrapped up his kingdom
in fathoms of chintz.

THE ISLAND OF LUNDY

The island of Lundy
is quiet on Sund'y
and not very lively
on Thursd'y and Mond'y.
Folks come from as far
as Goosebay and Fundy
to do nothing at all
on the island of Lundy.

LAZY LUCY

Lazy Lucy
lay in bed.
Lazy Lucy's
mother said:
"You will drive
your mother crazy.
Upsy-daisy,
Lucy Lazy!"
To her mom
said Lazy Lucy,
"Little children
can't be choosy
(though I would
prefer to snooze
in my bed
if I could choose).

I will not
drive Mamma crazy,
I will not
at all be lazy,
I will jump
right out of bed
—and be Sleepy Lu
instead."

MR. MELTER

Winslow Melter
built a shelter,
patiently if helter-skelter.
In the lonely
upper reaches
of the dunes
along the beaches,
out of driftwood
but with care,
out of sight
he built his lair.
When they cried:
"Seclusive Melter!
Such an eyesore
is your shelter,
we shall tear it down
this day!"
Sadly,
he went far away.

PERFECT ARTHUR

"Nowhere in the world,"
said Arthur,
"nowhere in the world,"
said he,
"is a boy
as absolutely
*per*fectly
per*fect*
as me!"

"Or, on second thought,"
said Arthur,
as he caught his mother's eye,
"should I say,
as absolutely
*per*fectly
perf*ect*
as I?"

GLUK

Where in the world is Haparanda?
And where in the world is Gluk?
Haparanda is north-northeast of Buganda
(ninety days' journey from Peking by panda)
and is easily found
—with some luck—
on a map.
But where is Gluk?

There are people who never could find Svappavaara,
though it sits on a sizable rock
one thousand nine hundred miles from Bokara
(or nearly as far as from Wuch to Skutara)
and is easily reached
—by truck—
from Namdal.
But where is Gluk?

I know where to find Timbuktu and Tirana
and Wupperthal, Kiev, and Bangkok
and Zagreb and Lhasa and Lvov and Ljubljana,
Gdynia, Gdansk, and Flathead, Montana,
Saskatchewan, Pinsk,
and Jokkmokk!
But where in the world is Gluk?

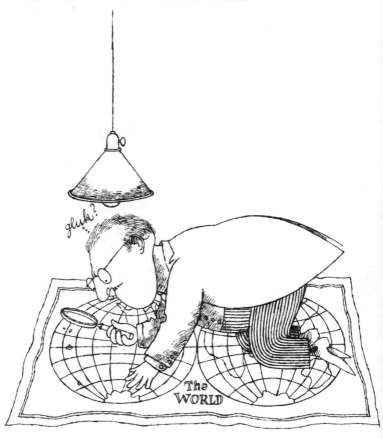

GETTING TOGETHER

Do you prefer
giblets to triplets,
or triplets to giblets,
or not?
Do you like carrots
as dearly as parrots,
or parrots far better,
or what?

Do you prefer
lizards to blizzards,
and blizzards and lizards
to lumps?
Do you like wrinkles
better than crinkles
and crinkles much better
than mumps?

Do you think slippers
are better than flippers,
and flippers are better
than flaps?
Then don't ever bother
to marry another.
We were meant for each other!
Perhaps.

Homer Beecher
(Spanish teacher)
taught his students
in a bleacher.
In the snows
that blow
and vanish,
in the rains
he taught them
Spanish,
till the students
went away
(went to proms
and far away).
When they told him:
"Mister Beecher,
durable
but frozen teacher,
not a soul is left.
Just look!"
Teacher Beecher
closed his book.